I0843867

CRYPTOGAME ACCOUNTS

REVEALING THE UNIVERSE OF GAMING ALTCOINS

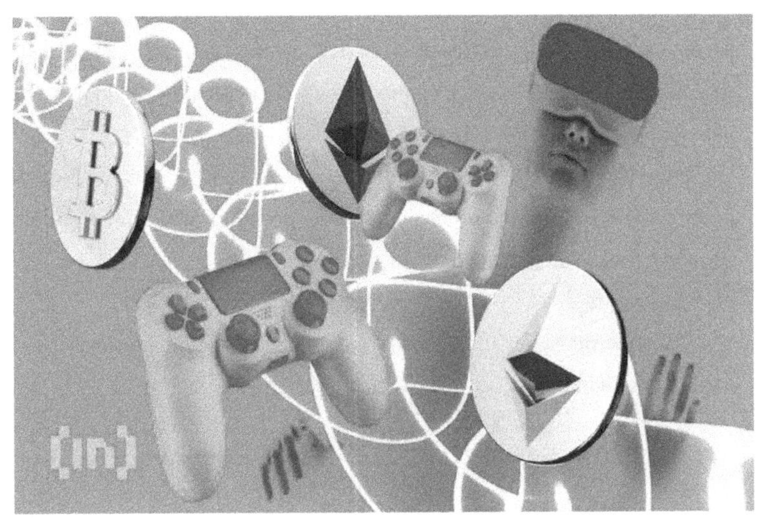

BY

JAMIU ADAM OPEYEMI

DEDICATION

I dedicate this book to God, whose divine guidance and grace have illuminated my path and granted me the strength and wisdom to embark on this journey of learning and growth. I am eternally grateful for the blessings and opportunities bestowed upon me.

To my parents, who have always been my pillars of support, love, and encouragement. Your unwavering belief in my abilities has fueled my determination to excel. Thank you for nurturing and shaping me into the person I am today.

To my well-wishers, whose words of encouragement, motivation, and belief in me have been a source of inspiration throughout this endeavor. Your faith in my capabilities has propelled me to strive for excellence, and for that, I extend my heartfelt gratitude.

May the outcomes of this book reflect the dedication and love I hold for each of you.

ACKNOWLEDGEMENTS

I would like to express my heartfelt gratitude to everyone who supported and encouraged me throughout this journey. First and foremost, I am deeply thankful for my family, whose unwavering love and understanding kept me grounded and motivated.

I am indebted to my friends and colleagues who provided valuable feedback and assistance in various aspects of this book. Their input was instrumental in refining the ideas and concepts presented in this book.

Lastly, I am immensely grateful to the readers, whose interest and enthusiasm for this book are the driving force behind my passion for writing.
Thank you all for being a part of this incredible journey.

JAMIU ADAM OPEYEMI

TABLE OF CONTENTS

LIST OF TABLES

Chapter 1: The Introduction of a Computerized Insurgency

- Prologue to the universe of cryptographic forms of money and their importance to gaming.

- A concise outline of the conventional gaming economy and its constraints.

- Genesis of the Ideas: How gaming altcoins turned into a reality.

Chapter 2: What Separates Gaming Altcoins

- Correlation with customary in-game monetary forms and government issued types of money.

- Advantags and Disadvantages of using gaming altcoins in virtual universes.

- Examples of well known gaming altcoins and their utilization cases.

Chapter 3: Building a Gaming Altcoin Environment

- The job of game designers in making and coordinating gaming altcoins.

- The effect of player networks in forming the gaming altcoin scene.

Chapter 4: The Gamification of Money

- How gaming components are integrated into monetary ideas inside the crypto-gaming biological system.

- Analysis of in-game economies and how they reflect certifiable monetary frameworks.

- The expected eventual fate of cross-stage economies, combining conventional money and gaming.

Chapter 5: Security and Risks in the Gaming Altcoin World

-Security concerns and vulnerabilities associated with gaming altcoins.

- Potential dangers like market unpredictability, tricks, and administrative difficulties.

- Methodologies to relieve gambles and guarantee a protected gaming altcoin experience.

Chapter 6: Coordinating Gaming Altcoins: Examples of overcoming adversity

- Contextual analyses of effective combination of gaming altcoins in different gaming stages.

- Interviews with developers, players, and influencers sharing their experiences and insights

- Lessons learned and best practices for integrating gaming altcoins effectively.

Chapter 7: The Future of Gaming Altcoins

- Foreseeing the future direction of gaming altcoins and their possible effect on the gaming business.

- Developments and forthcoming patterns forming the gaming altcoin scene.

- Hypotheses on how gaming altcoins could reclassify the eventual fate of gaming and money.

Conclusion: Unlocking the Virtual Vault

- Summing up key action points from the book.

- Empowering perusers to investigate the thrilling universe of gaming altcoins and imagine their future prospects.

CHAPTER ONE

THE INTRODUCTION OF A COMPUTERIZED UPHEAVAL

A. Prologue to the universe of cryptographic forms of money and their importance to gaming.

At the beginning of the 21st hundred years, another wave was peaking on the shores of the advanced scene, promising to reshape the actual groundwork of money and gaming. This extraordinary power arose as cryptographic forms of money, decentralized computerized monetary standards that were based on progressive innovation known as blockchain.

The idea of digital money sprang into existence with the making of Bitcoin in 2009 by a mysterious figure utilizing the pen name Nakamoto. Bitcoin acquainted the world with the possibility of a decentralized computerized cash, one that worked without a focal power, making exchanges secure, straightforward, and changeless.

As this momentous innovation built up forward movement, visionaries and trendsetters saw the likely past the monetary domain. They started investigating how digital currencies could reform different areas, and gaming stood apart as a superb contender for interruption. Gamers, long acclimated with virtual economies inside their gaming universes, began to see the capability of incorporating digital forms of money into their gaming encounters.

Digital currencies offered the possibility of genuine responsibility for game resources, empowering gamers to purchase, sell, and exchange virtual things safely and autonomously, without the requirement for delegates. This shift was a worldview jump, toppling conventional gaming models and giving players uncommon control and adaptability over their gaming resources.

In the mid-2000s, an idea arose that would before long change how we see worth and proprietorship in the computerized domain: digital forms of money. Bitcoin, the spearheading digital currency, was presented in 2009 by an unknown substance known as Satoshi Nakamoto. It was intended to be a decentralized computerized money, liberated from concentrated control and middle people like banks.

Around a similar time, the gaming business was encountering its development. Web-based gaming was getting forward momentum, and players were progressively associated with virtual economies, where in-game things and monetary forms held huge worth. Be that as it may, these virtual resources were kept to the domains of explicit games, constrained by game engineers, and needed genuine proprietorship.

Digital forms of money introduced an exceptional answer to this limit. The innovation that controlled Bitcoin, blockchain, was a decentralized and permanent record. It offered the capacity to tokenize resources, remembering for game things and monetary standards, giving them a certifiable worth and taking into consideration cross-game interoperability. This recently discovered combination of blockchain innovation and gaming established the groundwork for the prospering idea of "play-to-procure" gaming.

In the ensuing segments, we will dive further into how digital currencies and blockchain innovation have changed the gaming scene, setting out new open doors for players and reshaping the gaming business as far as we might be concerned. We will investigate the standards of blockchain innovation, the mechanics of tokenization, and the appearance of play-to-procure models. Moreover, we will talk about the difficulties and possible future improvements in this astonishing convergence of two unique domains. Go along with us as we uncover the introduction of a computerized upheaval, where gaming and digital forms of money entwine to reclassify the actual idea of play and possession.

Moreover, blockchain innovation, the fundamental foundation of digital currencies, considered the making of non-fungible tokens (NFTs), special computerized resources that could address anything from virtual land to uncommon in-game things. NFTs added a layer of proprietorship and credibility to the gaming experience, giving a feeling of shortage and worth beforehand concealed in the computerized domain.

The combination of gaming and cryptographic forms of money birthed another time when players were explorers in virtual domains as well as overseers of their advanced riches. The potential for genuine computerized proprietorship ignited enthusiasm inside the gaming local area, as lovers and designers the same started to imagine a future where games and virtual economies were consistently entwined with the decentralized force of digital currencies.

In the sections that follow, we will dig further into the significant effect of digital currencies on the gaming scene, investigating the advancement of this progressive association and the amazing potential it holds for the fate of the two enterprises. The introduction of this computerized upset denoted the start of an excursion that would everlastingly change how we play, own, and cooperate inside the tremendous domains of gaming.

B.   A concise outline of the conventional gaming economy and its constraints.

The customary gaming economy alludes to the procedure for purchasing, selling, and exchanging game things, cash, and administrations inside computer games. It includes certifiable exchanges, frequently worked with through stages, where players can buy virtual products utilizing genuine cash or procure in-game money through interactivity.

Nonetheless, this framework has a few limits. It, first and foremost, can prompt compensation to-win situations, where players with more discretionary cash flow can acquire a huge benefit over others. This sabotages fair rivalry and can prevent players from taking part in the game. Also, it can energize habit-forming spending designs, especially in games where in-game buys are intended to take advantage of mental triggers, possibly prompting monetary strain for certain people.

Moreover, the conventional gaming economy can cause a lopsidedness in the gaming local area, as not all players can stand to similarly partake. This can obstruct the general delight and inclusivity of the gaming experience. Finally, the auxiliary market for in-game things can need guidelines and might be defenceless to extortion or tricks, presenting takes a chance for the two purchasers and dealers.

Limitations include:

1. High Section Costs: Starting game buys or gaming equipment can be costly, restricting access for certain people.

2. Inequality of Access: Variations in admittance to gaming stages and high-velocity web can make a lopsided battleground.

3. Limited Adaptation Choices for Players: Gamers might find it hard to adapt their abilities and endeavours inside the conventional gaming model.

4. Depreciation and Resale Value: Actual games devalue in esteem over the long haul, and the resale market can be unstable.

5. Centralized Control: Distributers and stage proprietors apply huge command over game appropriation, estimating, and arrangements.

6. Lack of Transparency: The complexities of estimating, income circulation, and information use aren't generally straightforward to gamers.

7. Exclusivity and Fragmentation: Eliteness arrangements and stage discontinuity can prompt a separated player base and limited game access.

In outline, while the conventional gaming economy offers accommodation and adaptation potential to open doors, it delivers difficulties connected with reasonableness, enslavement, inclusivity, and security.

C. Genesis of the Ideas: How gaming altcoins turned into a reality.

The beginning of gaming altcoins follows back to the developing prevalence of digital forms of money and the advancing gaming industry. As blockchain innovation built up some momentum for its security and straightforwardness, aficionados saw a chance to consolidate it with gaming. This combination considered the making of remarkable in-game resources, decentralized commercial centres, and imaginative approaches to boost players. Over the long run, committed projects arose, spearheading the idea of gaming altcoins and displaying the potential for another financial biological system inside the gaming scene.

The rise of gaming altcoins can be credited to a union of elements in the digital money and gaming domains. The beginning of this thought originates from the developing prevalence of digital forms of money and the exceptional requirements inside the gaming local area.

1. Cryptocurrency Blast and Innovation: With the ascent of Bitcoin and later Ethereum, the world saw the capability of blockchain innovation past monetary exchanges. The hidden blockchain innovation is considered decentralized, straightforward, and secure exchanges, rousing development in different ventures.

2. Monetization in Gaming: In the gaming business, designers and players looked for imaginative ways of adapting the gaming experience. Conventional in-game buys, memberships, and notices were pervasive, however, they frequently accompanied limits and unified control.

3. Smart Agreements and Tokens: Ethereum's presentation of savvy contracts and the capacity to make custom tokens gave an impetus. Shrewd agreements empowered self-executing contracts with the terms straightforwardly composed into code, considering trustless exchanges and mechanized processes.

4. Gaming People group and Virtual Economies: Gamers have for some time been essential for assorted, dynamic networks inside games, frequently including virtual economies. Things, monetary standards, and resources acquired esteem through shortage and request, making way for tokenization.

5. Tokenization of In-Game Assets: Tokenization permitted gaming resources to be addressed as exceptional tokens on a blockchain, conceding proprietorship and empowering exchange. This idea was progressive, as it worked with genuine responsibility for game things and possibly opened up new income streams.

6. Initial Coin Contributions (ICOs): Propelled by the outcome of ICOs in the cryptographic money space, gaming projects started to investigate ICOs as a way to finance their drives. This gathering pledges model considered the assortment of assets from a more extensive base of financial backers.

7. Gaming Altcoins Ecosystem: The thought developed further with the making of explicit altcoins customized to the gaming business. These altcoins were intended to be utilized inside gaming environments, controlling in-game exchanges, giving motivators, and empowering a consistent virtual economy.

8. Integration of Gaming Altcoins: Game designers saw the capability of coordinating gaming altcoins into their foundation to upgrade player commitment, faithfulness, and income. These altcoins offered remarkable highlights like prizes, casting ballot rights, and administration inside the gaming local area.

The conjunction of blockchain innovation, the requirement for decentralized in-game economies, and the ascent of digital currencies prepared for gaming altcoins. These computerized resources have fundamentally influenced the gaming business, giving new open doors to both gamers and engineers to partake in a more comprehensive and creative virtual climate.

CHAPTER TWO

WHAT SEPARATES GAMING ALTCOINS

D. Correlation with customary in-game monetary forms and government-issued types of money.

In the realm of gaming, money has consistently assumed a vital part. It is the soul of virtual economies, working with exchanges inside gaming conditions. Generally, in-game monetary forms have been controlled and overseen by game designers, firmly coordinated into the gaming biological system. These monetary forms frequently have restricted use and worth, limited exclusively to explicit games or stages.

Gaming altcoins, a particular class of cryptographic money, have acquired noticeable quality inside the gaming business in light of multiple factors. To comprehend their uniqueness, a correlation between conventional in-game monetary standards and government-issued types of money is fundamental.

Customary in-game monetary standards are normally restricted to the particular gaming climate, binding their utilization and worth inside the actual game. They need interoperability and can't be used past the gaming biological system. Then again, gaming altcoins frequently influence blockchain innovation, giving them qualities similar to customary digital currencies like Bitcoin and Ethereum. This empowers cross-game similarity and possibly stretches out their utilization to different applications past gaming.

Also, customary in-game monetary forms are generally unified and constrained by the game designers, permitting them to control the cash's worth and supply. Interestingly, gaming altcoins, based on decentralized blockchain networks, work on straightforward and changeless conventions, encouraging trust and forestalling unnecessary impact on their worth.

When contrasted with government-issued types of money, gaming altcoins share specific benefits. Government-issued types of money are vulnerable to expansion, devaluation, and financial vacillations impacted by government arrangements and monetary circumstances. Gaming altcoins, using blockchain and a limited stockpile, frequently offer dependability concerning esteem conservation, adding to a more unsurprising financial climate inside the gaming biological system.

Then again, government-issued types of money, similar to the US dollar or the Euro, have a more extensive degree and capability outside the gaming domain. They are dependent upon unofficial laws and national bank strategies, affecting their worth and soundness. Clients can utilize government-issued types of money across different areas, not simply in gaming.

Fiat exchanges include middle people like banks, bringing about expenses and postponements. Gaming altcoins, utilizing blockchain's decentralized nature, work with speedier and savvy exchanges, further developing the general client experience.

Gaming altcoins, nonetheless, present an alternate worldview. They are decentralized, frequently founded on blockchain innovation, taking into account shared exchanges without the requirement for go-betweens. This decentralization awards gamers more control and responsibility for virtual resources and cash. Moreover, gaming altcoins can frequently be utilized across different games or even exchanged on different digital currency trades, giving them natural worth past a particular gaming climate.

Besides, the shortage and limited supply of many gaming altcoins emulate certifiable financial standards, cultivating requests and possibly valuing in esteem over the long haul. This stands rather than customary in-game monetary standards, which can be dependent upon expansion or emptying at the caution of game engineers.

Gaming altcoins separate themselves from customary in-game monetary standards and government-issued types of money by utilizing decentralization, more extensive convenience, potential for esteem appreciation, and similarity to certifiable financial elements. These highlights add to a developing scene where virtual monetary forms are turning out to be progressively huge and powerful in the gaming business.

E. Advantages and Disadvantages of using gaming altcoins in virtual universes.

Gaming altcoins, otherwise called digital currencies intended for gaming stages or virtual universes, offer exceptional benefits and detriments.

ADVANTAGES:

1. Decentralization and Ownership: Gaming altcoins work on decentralized blockchain networks, conceding players genuine responsibility for game resources and money, encouraging a feeling of pride and control.

2. Interoperability and Cross-Stage Transactions: Using gaming altcoins empowers consistent exchanges and resource moves across different games and stages, upgrading client encounters and cultivating a bound-together gaming environment.

3. Monetization and Monetary Incentives: Players can acquire, exchange, or buy gaming altcoins, setting out open doors for monetary benefits inside the virtual world. This boosts dynamic investment and ability improvement.

4. In-Game Exchanges and Microtransactions: Gaming altcoins work with proficient microtransactions for in-game buys, improving the general ongoing interaction experience by giving a fast and secure instalment strategy.

DISADVANTAGES:

1. Price Unpredictability and Speculative Nature: The benefit of gaming altcoins can be exceptionally unstable, representing a gamble for players who put resources into them. Abrupt value changes can prompt significant misfortunes or gains, influencing the gaming economy.

2. Complexity and Learning Curve: Getting it and overseeing digital currencies can be overwhelming for certain clients, preventing likely reception because of the specialized information expected to explore and use gaming altcoins successfully.

3. Security Dangers and Hacking: Digital currencies and blockchain networks are defenceless to hacking and security breaks. In-game resources and speculations can be compromised, prompting monetary misfortunes and doubt inside the gaming local area.

4. Dependency on Blockchain Infrastructure: The adequacy of gaming altcoins depends on the basic blockchain's solidness and versatility. Network clogs or specialized issues can disturb exchanges and interactivity, influencing the client experience.

While gaming altcoins offer likely advantages concerning possession, interoperability, and financial motivators, they likewise present difficulties connected with cost instability, intricacy, security dangers, and reliance on blockchain framework. Cautious thought of these perspectives is significant for the two engineers and players while integrating gaming altcoins into virtual universes.

F. Examples of well-known gaming altcoins and their utilization cases.

As of September 2021, well-known gaming altcoins and their utilization cases up to that point. Notwithstanding, if it's not too much trouble, note that the digital currency scene is exceptionally unique, and new tasks might have arisen or advanced from that point forward.

1. Enjin Coin (ENJ)

Enjin Coin is intended to be coordinated into gaming environments, permitting engineers to make and oversee in-game resources on the blockchain. It works with proprietorship, provenance, and worth of virtual things, making them tradable across various games.

2. Chiliz (CHZ)

Chiliz is a blockchain stage for sports and diversion, including gaming. It empowers sports and gaming associations to tokenize fan commitment and deal with tradable advanced resources, upgrading fan inclusion and making new income streams.

3. The Sandbox (SAND)

The Sandbox is a virtual world-building game and stage that utilizes blockchain to empower players to possess, make, and adapt their gaming encounters. SAND is utilized for exchanges inside the biological system and for buying virtual resources.

4. Decentraland (MANA)

Decentraland is a decentralized computer-generated simulation stage where clients can make, insight, and adapt content and applications. MANA is utilized to trade virtual land, things, and administrations inside the stage.

5. Axie Boundlessness (AXS)

Axie Boundlessness is a blockchain-based game where players can gather, breed, and fight dream animals called Axies. AXS is utilized for administration, marking, and partaking in the environment.

6. Theta Token (THETA)

Theta Token is a blockchain explicitly intended for video web-based and esports. It boosts clients to share their data transmission and assets, working on the quality and proficiency of video web-based, which can be pertinent for gaming streams and esports.

CHAPTER THREE

BUILDING A GAMING ALTCOIN ENVIRONMENT

G. The Job Of Game Designers Is To Make And Coordinate Gaming Altcoins.

In the domain of digital currency and gaming, the coordination of gaming altcoins has arisen as an urgent pattern, reshaping how players communicate with virtual universes. This joining wouldn't be imaginable without the proactive job of game designer who have an urgent impact in making and flawlessly coordinating these altcoins into the gaming biological system.

Game designers, the draftsmen behind the virtual universes, are instrumental in imagining and planning altcoins custom-fitted for explicit games. These altcoins, frequently alluded to as in-game tokens or coins, act as a vehicle of trade inside the game climate. The designers fastidiously characterize the characteristics, supply cap, and utility of these altcoins, adjusting them to the game's elements and story.

Moreover, game designers assemble the framework fundamental for these altcoins to work inside the game, frequently utilizing blockchain innovation. This innovation not only guarantees the security and changelessness of exchanges yet in addition empowers proprietorship and exchange of in-game resources outside the game climate. Brilliant agreements, a central part of the blockchain, oversee exchanges, proprietorship moves, and other in-game collaborations, enabling players with genuine responsibility for virtual effects.

The combination of gaming altcoins makes another layer of commitment, permitting players to procure rewards and exchange resources in a decentralized and straightforward way. Game designer influence this by inserting creative ongoing interaction instruments that boost players to use and exchange these altcoins. Through this, an energetic in-game economy is sustained, drawing local gamers and lovers.

Joint efforts between game designer and blockchain projects further fuel the reconciliation of gaming altcoins. Joint endeavours bring specialized mastery and a more extensive client base, encouraging the development and reception of altcoins in the gaming scene. Furthermore, these coordinated efforts lead to the advancement of interoperable stages, empowering players to use their resources across different games and biological systems.

All in all, game designer assume a vital part in the creation and mix of gaming altcoins. Their vision, specialized ability, and cooperation endeavours with blockchain projects prepare for a thriving gaming altcoin biological system, enabling players and reclassifying the fate of gaming.

H. The Effect of Player Networks in Forming the Gaming Altcoin Scene

Player people groups have essentially affected the gaming altcoin scene, their effect appearing in different ways. These people frequently capability as early adopters, supporting and putting resources into gaming-related altcoins. Their aggregate impact can decisively influence the worth and view of these altcoins, adding to showcase patterns.

Right off the bat, player networks assume a pivotal part in the underlying turn of events and advancement of gaming altcoins. Energetic gamers, understanding the expected advantages of blockchain innovation for gaming, effectively participate in conversations, gatherings, and virtual entertainment stages, upholding the combination of explicit altcoins inside their favoured games.

In addition, these networks give important criticism to engineers, assisting with refining and designing altcoins to fulfil the novel needs of gamers. Engineers frequently effectively take part in these networks, acquiring experiences into the inclinations and prerequisites of their interest group, hence directing the further improvement of the altcoin.

Gaming altcoins frequently integrate highlights like non-fungible tokens (NFTs) and decentralized finance (DeFi) components, cooking explicitly for gamers. Player people group, being profoundly drenched in the gaming society, relate to and promptly embrace these altcoins. Their underwriting encourages broad reception inside the gaming local area.

Moreover, player networks add to the reception of gaming altcoins by going about as early adopters and making an organisational impact. As individuals from the local area use and execute the altcoin inside their gaming environment, they urge others to do likewise. This natural development prompts a more extensive acknowledgement of the altcoin inside the gaming local area and then some.

At times, player networks start or effectively take part in the advancement of altcoins, utilizing their ability and enthusiasm for gaming. Such contribution hardens the cooperative connection between gaming and digital money networks, forming the gaming altcoin scene.

By and large, player networks use significant impact in the gaming altcoin scene, guiding the bearing of improvement, reception, and worth through their energetic commitment and underwriting.

CHAPTER FOUR

THE GAMIFICATION OF MONEY

I. How Gaming Components are Integrated into Monetary Ideas Inside the Crypto-gaming Biological System.

In the quickly developing scene of money, the mixture of gaming components has reformed how monetary ideas are drawn closer, especially inside the crypto-gaming environment. This converging of two unmistakable domains has brought forth another worldview, where monetary exercises and gaming standards amicably coincide, taking care of a different crowd anxious to draw in with the two spaces.

The mix of gaming components into monetary ideas inside the crypto-gaming environment essentially appears through a few key systems:

1. Incentivization and Prizes Systems

In customary money, motivations frequently come as financing costs or profits. Be that as it may, in the crypto-gaming environment, this is gamified by utilizing reward frameworks suggestive of in-game accomplishments. Members are boosted through tokens, NFTs (Non-Fungible Tokens), or other virtual resources, empowering them to connect all the more effectively.

2. Tokenization and Resource Ownership

Tokenization, a critical part of digital forms of money, reflects the idea of in-game resources in the gaming scene. Every token addresses proprietorship or worth, likened to how in-game things give specific capacities or worth inside a game. This component cultivates a feeling of pride and commitment, like the fervour of possessing uncommon in-game things.

3. Competitive Components and Leaderboards

Integrating cutthroat angles with lists of competitors, rankings, or competitions brings the appeal of gaming into monetary exercises. Clients can vie for remunerations in light of their exhibition, improving commitment and advancing pride.

4. Interactive UIs and Client Experience

The crypto-gaming environment frequently utilizes instinctive and outwardly engaging connection points, much the same as gaming connection points. This improves the client experience, making monetary collaborations seriously captivating and available, drawing in both prepared and new members.

5. Narrative and Storytelling

Accounts and narrating, unmistakable in gaming, are utilized to pass on monetary data and systems in a connecting with way. By making convincing stories, clients can connect with monetary ideas better and understand complex data all the more without any problem.

6. Quests and Challenges

Carrying out journeys or difficulties, much the same as gaming missions gamifies the learning and reception of monetary ideas. Clients are directed through a progression of undertakings or difficulties, improving their comprehension and capability in dealing with their monetary portfolios.

7. Real-Time Input and Progress Tracking

Giving constant input on monetary choices and showing progress similar to gaming progress bars or level-ups builds up client commitment. This prompt input circle propels clients to take an interest and further develop their monetary techniques effectively.

The combination of gaming components with finance inside the crypto-gaming biological system has opened up astonishing potential outcomes. This intermingling not only draws in a more youthful and more educated crowd but also democratizes finance, making it more open, intuitive, and pleasant for all. As this incorporation keeps on developing, it holds the possibility to reclassify conventional monetary frameworks, making an energetic and dynamic monetary scene.

J. Analysis of In-game Economies and How They Reflect Certifiable Monetary Frameworks.

In-game economies frequently reflect true monetary frameworks in more than one way. They ordinarily have money (e.g., gold, credits) and an arrangement of the organic market that influences costs. In-game creation, exchange, and utilization look like certifiable financial exercises, and players can aggregate abundance through different means. Furthermore, expansion, market control, and monetary disparities can be seen in both in-game and genuine economies, impacting interactivity and player collaborations.

These equals should be visible through a few key viewpoints:

1. Currency and Worth Exchange

In the two domains, there is a characterized unit of trade (cash) and systems for esteem move. Very much like certifiable monetary forms, in-game monetary standards can change in light of supply, request, and in-game occasions.

2. Supply and Request Dynamics

In-game economies show organic market standards, affecting thing costs. Scant or appealing things will quite often have higher worth, like wares in reality.

3. Marketplaces and Trading

Game commercial centres, similar to stock trades, permit players to purchase, sell, and exchange virtual resources. This connection makes a market biological system with its patterns, theory, and cost changes.

4. Inflation and Deflation

In-game economies can encounter expansion because of an oversupply of money or emptying because of shortage. Engineers might manage these through changes, reflecting national bank mediations in reality.

5. Investments and Speculation

Players frequently put resources into virtual resources, theorizing on future worth. This mirrors certifiable venture systems and monetary business sectors where members look for profits from their speculations.

6. Regulation and Oversight

Game engineers go about as controllers, changing game mechanics to keep a reasonable economy. This job is likened to a national bank's liability in dealing with a country's financial strategy.

7. Economic Policies

Game designers execute financial arrangements like assessment frameworks, punishments, or rewards to impact player conduct, similar to how states carry out monetary and money-related approaches to shape true economies.

8. Economic Development and Development

In-game economies might encounter development as new players join or through game extensions, comparable to monetary development in nations because of populace increments or mechanical progressions.

9. Social and Mental Factors

Similarly, as certifiable discernments and social patterns impact monetary business sectors, player conduct, networks, and patterns inside the game can essentially affect the in-game economy.

Understanding and concentrating on these equals enhances how we might interpret virtual economies as well as reveals insight into certifiable financial standards in a clever setting.

K. The Expected Eventual Fate of Cross-stage Economies, Combining Conventional Money and Gaming.

In the possible fate of cross-stage economies, we imagine a consistent mix of conventional money and gaming, making a powerful biological system where virtual and genuine economies entwine. Envision a reality where in-game resources hold substantial worth and can be exchanged in monetary business sectors. Players could procure genuine pay through their gaming exercises, utilizing blockchain innovation to guarantee the possession and validity of virtual resources. This union could alter ventures and open doors, permitting gamers to differentiate portfolios past conventional resources. The limit between gaming and money would obscure, opening up interesting opportunities for another period of interconnected economies.

The expected fate of cross-stage economies holds massive commitment, imagining a consistent incorporation of customary money and gaming domains. This assembly is filled by the developing fame of virtual economies inside computer games and the longing to connect these virtual resources with certifiable monetary frameworks.

In this imagined future, blockchain innovation assumes a significant part. The execution of blockchain considers secure and straightforward exchanges, empowering players to claim and exchange their in-game resources genuinely. Non-fungible tokens (NFTs) become a basic part, addressing interesting computerized things inside games. These NFTs can be purchased, sold, or even utilized as security in monetary exchanges.

Besides, decentralized finance (DeFi) conventions will coordinate with gaming stages, permitting players to take part in loaning, acquiring, and marketing utilizing their in-game resources as a guarantee. Shrewd agreements work with mechanized payouts and implement rules, guaranteeing a trustless and productive framework.

Interoperability between various games and stages will be a key concentration, empowering clients to involve their resources across different games or even in the more extensive monetary environment. Cross-stage resource moves and exchanges will make an energetic and interconnected economy, rising above the limits of individual games.

Guidelines and legitimate structures will advance to address the intricacies of this crossover biological system, guaranteeing purchaser assurance, charge consistency, and fair play. Industry joint effort and principles will arise to work with this development and encourage inescapable reception.

The fate of cross-stage economies consolidating conventional money and gaming presents a thrilling scene of potential, mixing gaming commitment with genuine monetary open doors through blockchain, NFTs, DeFi coordination, and administrative structures.

CHAPTER FIVE

SECURITY AND RISKS IN THE GAMING ALTCOIN WORLD

L. Security Concerns And Vulnerabilities Associated With Gaming Altcoins.

Gaming altcoins have gained traction in the cryptocurrency space, offering unique features and experiences within the gaming community. However, like any emerging technology, they come with their own set of security concerns and vulnerabilities that need to be addressed. Here, we'll delve into some of the key aspects of security and risks associated with gaming altcoins. This chapter delves into the various security concerns and vulnerabilities that are characteristic of the gaming altcoin ecosystem.

1. Smart Contract Vulnerabilities

Gaming altcoins often utilize smart contracts to facilitate in-game transactions and functions. However, these contracts can be susceptible to bugs, exploits, and vulnerabilities, leading to potential losses and disruptions in gameplay.

2. Double-Spending Attacks

The risk of double-spending attacks is heightened in gaming altcoins due to the frequent and rapid transactions within the gaming environment. Malicious actors may attempt to spend the same coins multiple times, disrupting the fairness and integrity of the gaming system.

3. Phishing and Social Engineering

Gamers may fall victim to phishing attempts or social engineering, leading to the compromise of their private keys or wallet information. Hackers can deceive users into revealing sensitive data, resulting in unauthorized access and theft.

4. Centralized Exchanges and Security Risks

Many gaming altcoins are traded on centralized exchanges, posing risks such as hacking, insider threats, and security breaches. Exchange compromises can result in significant losses for both gamers and investors.

5. Lack of Regulation and Consumer Protections

The gaming altcoin market often operates in a regulatory grey area. The absence of clear regulations can leave gamers vulnerable to fraudulent schemes, scams, and inadequate legal protections.

6. Sybil Attacks

Sybil attacks involve creating a large number of nodes to gain control or disrupt a network. In gaming altcoins, this can undermine the fairness of in-game events and competitions, negatively impacting the overall gaming experience.

7. Third-Party Integration Risks

Gaming altcoins frequently integrate with third-party platforms and technologies. These integrations may introduce vulnerabilities, as the security measures of external platforms might not align with the level of security required in the gaming altcoin ecosystem.

8. Market Volatility and Speculative Risks

The inherent volatility of cryptocurrency markets can impact the value of gaming altcoins. Sudden price fluctuations can lead to financial losses for investors and impact the perceived value of in-game assets.

To address these security concerns and risks, a multi-faceted approach involving robust smart contract auditing, education and awareness campaigns for gamers, enhanced regulatory frameworks, decentralized exchanges, and security-focused development practices is imperative. Collaboration among developers, gamers, and regulatory bodies is crucial to fostering a secure and trustworthy gaming altcoin environment.

M. Potential Dangers Like Market Unpredictability, Tricks, and Administrative Difficulties.

Putting resources into monetary business sectors conveys innate dangers, like market unpredictability where costs can change capriciously. Furthermore, tricks and fake plans represent a threat to financial backers, requiring alert and a reasonable level of effort.

Market unpredictability, tricks, and administrative difficulties present huge dangers in different spaces.

Market unpredictability alludes to quick and critical cost changes inside monetary business sectors, making speculations unusual and possibly prompting significant misfortunes for financial backers.

Tricks inside venture markets include deceitful plans or exercises intended to bamboozle financial backers, bringing about monetary misfortune or burglary of assets. These tricks frequently exploit falsehood or absence of information in financial backers.

Administrative difficulties include the advancing and complex guidelines forced by states and administering bodies. Changes in approaches can affect ventures, expecting organizations to adjust quickly or face legitimate results.

Tending to these dangers requires exhaustive exploration, risk evaluation, broadening of speculations, remaining informed about market patterns, and consistency with important guidelines. Also, looking for exhortation from monetary experts can support exploring these possible entanglements.

Moreover, administrative changes and difficulties can affect ventures, highlighting the significance of remaining educated and versatile in the monetary scene.

N.   Methodologies To Relieve Gambles And Guarantee A Protected Gaming Altcoin Experience.

Guaranteeing a safe gaming altcoin experience includes a complex methodology that tends to likely dangerous. Here are methodologies to relieve dangers and upgrade security:

1. Thorough Due Diligence

A direct broad exploration of the gaming altcoin, its improvement group, whitepaper, local area commitment, and by and large task guide. Search for believability and straightforwardness.

2. Secure Wallets

Utilize trustworthy and secure wallets to store your gaming altcoins. Equipment wallets are viewed as the most reliable choice, trailed by respectable programming wallets with solid encryption.

3. Two-Authenticator Validation (2FA)

Carry out 2FA in any place conceivable to add a layer of safety to your records, making it harder for unapproved access.

4. Regular Programming Updates

Guarantee that your wallet programming, working framework, and antivirus programs are in the know regarding the most recent security fixes and updates.

5. Phishing Awareness

Be watchful about phishing endeavours. Never share your confidential keys, seed expressions, or individual data through dubious connections or messages.

6. Beware of Scams

Remain careful of plans promising ensured returns or dubious speculation valuable open doors connected with the gaming altcoin. Confirm the authenticity of undertakings before taking an interest.

7. Multi-Mark Transactions

Consider utilizing multi-signature exchanges, where various confidential keys are expected to approve an exchange, adding an additional layer of safety.

8. Limit Exposure

Abstain from uncovering a lot of your gaming altcoins on trades. Just save the important sum for exchanging or exchanges, and move the rest to a solid wallet.

9. Educate Yourself

Constantly instruct yourself on developing security dangers and best practices inside the digital currency and blockchain space.

10. Strong Passwords

Utilize complex passwords and think about utilizing a secret key chief to produce and safely store them.

11. Network Security

Guarantee your organization and gadgets are secure by utilizing firewalls, routinely refreshing firmware, and utilizing antivirus programming.

12. Stay Informed

Join legitimate networks and follow confided-in hotspots for updates and news about the gaming altcoin. Remain informed about any potential security weaknesses or concerns.

By joining these systems, you can essentially decrease the dangers related to purchasing and utilizing gaming altcoins while partaking in a safer encounter.

CHAPTER SIX

COORDINATING GAMING ALTCOINS: EXAMPLES OF OVERCOMING ADVERSITY

O. Contextual Analyses Of An Effective Combination Of Gaming Altcoins In Different Gaming Stages.

Lately, the coordination of gaming altcoins into different gaming stages has gotten some decent momentum, introducing novel open doors for both gamers and the cryptographic money local area. In this part, we will investigate a few examples of overcoming adversity displaying the consistent coordination of gaming altcoins, their effect on the gaming business, and the advantages they proposition to the gaming biological system.

1. Enjin Coin (ENJ) and Minecraft

Enjin Coin, a digital currency custom-made for the gaming business, has seen huge progress in coordinating with one of the world's most famous games, Minecraft. Enjin laid out a blockchain-based resource proprietorship framework, permitting players to make, exchange, and oversee in-game things safely. This mix has empowered players to genuinely possess their in-game resources, cultivating a flourishing player-driven economy inside Minecraft.

2. Decentraland (MANA) and Virtual Real Estate

Decentraland, a computer-generated simulation stage, utilizes its local digital money, MANA, to influence a decentralized environment where clients can purchase, sell, and foster virtual land. This spearheading idea has prompted a roaring virtual housing market, drawing in both gamers and financial backers. The effective combination of MANA has made an interesting virtual existence where proprietorship and exchanges are recorded on the blockchain.

3. Theta (THETA) and Theta Fuel (TFUEL) in Streaming Services

Theta Organization has presented THETA and TFUEL, digital currencies intended to change video in real time. By incorporating these altcoins, Theta Organization boosts clients to share their transmission capacity and add to the decentralized streaming organization. Gamers can procure TFUEL by watching or sharing their interactivity, giving a creative method for adapting gaming content.

4. WAX (WAXP) and Virtual Item Trading

The Overall Resource Trade (WAX) has effectively incorporated its local token, WAXP, into different gaming stages. WAX works with secure and productive exchanging of virtual things, permitting gamers to purchase, sell, and exchange game resources across various games and stages. This interoperability has upgraded the gaming experience and enhanced the gaming economy.

These examples of overcoming adversity exhibit the capability of incorporating gaming altcoins into gaming stages, opening new roads for development, proprietorship, and adaptation inside the gaming environment. As the cryptographic money scene keeps on developing, we can expect further progressions and inventive mixes that will shape the eventual fate of gaming.

P. Interviews With Developers, Players, and Influencers Sharing their Experiences and Insights

Title: "Unveiling the Chronicles of Gaming: A Saga of Experiences and Insights"

Introduction:

In the realm of gaming, a multitude of experiences and insights shape the landscape. Developers, players, and influencers have traversed this digital odyssey, each contributing to the tapestry of the gaming world. In this immersive narrative, we delve into their stories, recounting the events and revelations that unfolded in the ever-evolving domain of gaming.

Interview 1: Developer's Tale - Crafting Dreams

[Developer Name]

[Game Title/Company]

Q: How did you venture into game development?

A: My journey began with a childhood passion for gaming. The allure of creating worlds and stories led me to pursue a career in game development. Joining [Company Name] allowed me to craft my dreams into playable experiences.

Q: What challenges did you face during development?

A: Balancing creativity and technical constraints was a persistent challenge. Striking that delicate equilibrium between innovation and feasibility often demanded arduous iterations and decision-making.

Q: How does player feedback influence your projects?

A: Player feedback is the lifeblood of our development process. We meticulously analyze player reviews, forums, and social media to refine our games. Their insights guide us in enhancing gameplay, addressing bugs, and incorporating features that resonate with our audience.

Interview 2: Player's Odyssey - A Digital Chronicle
[Player Name]
[Gamer Tag]

Q: When did your gaming journey commence?
A: My gaming journey commenced in the early 2000s with my first console. It quickly evolved into a passion, offering an escape into fantastical realms and thrilling adventures.

Q: What drives your passion for gaming?
A: Gaming is a form of art and storytelling. The immersion, the challenges, and the social connections it offers are unparalleled. It's a dynamic medium that keeps me constantly engaged and excited.

Q: How has gaming influenced your life outside the virtual world?
A: Gaming has instilled problem-solving skills, teamwork, and creativity in my life. It's also a source of cherished friendships, as I've met incredible individuals through gaming communities.

Interview 3: Influencer Chronicles - Forging a Digital Empire
[Influencer Name]
[YouTube/Twitch Channel]

Q: How did you venture into the world of gaming content creation?

A: I started my journey by sharing my gaming experiences on platforms like YouTube and Twitch. The community's positive response encouraged me to delve deeper, and eventually, it turned into a full-fledged channel.

Q: What challenges did you face in building your gaming community?
A: The initial challenge was gaining visibility and establishing credibility. Building a loyal audience required consistent content creation and engaging with my viewers. Overcoming these hurdles was incredibly rewarding.

Q: How do you perceive your role as a gaming influencer?
A: I see myself as a bridge between developers and players. My role is to entertain, educate, and provide valuable insights to my audience. It's about creating a symbiotic relationship that benefits both parties and contributes to the gaming ecosystem.

Conclusion:

Through these diverse perspectives, we unravel the multifaceted nature of gaming. Developers, players, and influencers are interconnected, each playing a vital role in shaping this ever-evolving digital universe. Their experiences and insights pave the way for the future of gaming, fostering innovation, and enriching the gaming landscape for generations to come.

Q. Lessons Learned And Best Practices For Integrating Gaming Altcoins Effectively.

Integrating gaming altcoins effectively includes cautious preparation and execution. Here are a few vital illustrations and best practices to accomplish a fruitful combination:

1. Understanding the Gaming Community

Research and appreciate the gaming local area's inclinations, ways of behaving, and assumptions connected with in-game economies and virtual monetary standards.

2. Establish Clear Objectives

Characterize explicit objectives for coordinating altcoins, for example, upgrading interactivity, empowering in-game buys, or making a player-driven economy.

3. Selecting the Right Altcoin

- Pick a gaming altcoin that lines up with the game's subject, ideal interest group, and objectives. Consider factors like exchange speed, charges, and mix ease.

4. Seamless Integration

Guarantee a smooth and instinctive reconciliation of the altcoin inside the game to give a consistent client experience. Execute simple to-involve wallets and clear guidelines for exchanges.

5. Incentivize Usage

Foster systems to boost players to utilize the altcoin, for example, select in-game prizes, limits, or rewards for utilizing the digital currency.

6. Educational Resources

Give instructive assets inside the game to teach players the most proficient method to utilize the altcoin, its advantages, and the way that it upgrades their gaming experience.

7. Community Engagement

Cultivate major areas of strength around the altcoin coordination by empowering conversations, and criticism, and including players in dynamic connected with the in-game economy.

8. Security Measures

Carry out vigorous safety efforts to protect players' exchanges, resources, and information. Consistently update security conventions to remain in front of expected dangers.

9. Monitoring and Analytics

Use examination to follow altcoin use designs, player commitment, and exchange patterns. This information can illuminate acclimations to the incorporation technique for ideal outcomes.

10. Regulatory Compliance

Guarantee consistency with applicable gaming and monetary guidelines, including information protection regulations and monetary revealing prerequisites related to utilizing digital money.

11. Scalability and Flexibility

Construct a mix that can scale with the development of the game and adjust to advancing innovation and market patterns in the digital currency space.

12. Feedback Loop

Lay out an input circle with players to gather their perspectives, concerns, and ideas regarding the altcoin mix. Utilize this criticism to make informed upgrades.

13. Collaborations and Partnerships

Investigate cooperation valuable open doors with other gaming ventures or stages that utilise the equivalent altcoin, possibly making a more extensive biological system for the digital money inside the gaming business.

By following these illustrations and best practices, game designers can incorporate gaming altcoins, upgrading the gaming experience and driving commitment inside their player networks.

CHAPTER SEVEN
THE FUTURE OF GAMING ALTCOINS

R. Foreseeing The Future Direction Of Gaming Altcoins And Their Possible Effect On The Gaming Business.

In this part, we dive into the charming domain of gaming altcoins and investigate their capability to alter the gaming business. Altcoins, or elective digital currencies to Bitcoin, have built up some decent momentum as of late. In particular, gaming altcoins are advanced monetary forms intended to be coordinated into gaming biological systems, offering different advantages to gamers, designers, and distributors.

As we stand on the cliff of another period in the gaming business, set apart by the ascent of blockchain innovation and decentralized finance (DeFi), gaming altcoins are rising as a significant player in this extraordinary scene. These computerized monetary standards, based on blockchain networks, offer remarkable open doors for both gamers and engineers, possibly reshaping how we see and draw in with computer games.

1. The Assembly of Gaming and Blockchain

Gaming altcoins are at the crossing point of two quickly developing spaces - gaming and blockchain. Blockchain innovation offers highlights like straightforwardness, security, and proprietorship freedoms through non-fungible tokens (NFTs), giving a promising establishment to the gaming business. This combination opens up new roads for decentralized gaming, empowering genuine responsibility for game resources and economies.

2. Empowering Gamers

One of the critical effects of gaming altcoins is the strengthening of gamers. By using blockchain, players can possess their in-game resources, guaranteeing interoperability across different games and stages. This encourages a feeling of responsibility as well as presents a potential financial aspect where players can exchange, sell, or adapt their computerized resources outside the game environment.

3. Fostering Decentralized Economies

Gaming altcoins can work with the making of decentralized gaming economies, where gamers and engineers can connect straightforwardly through shrewd agreements and decentralized applications (dApps). These economies could boost gamers for their accomplishments, commitments, and in-game activities, at last, driving commitment and making a self-supporting environment.

4. Innovative Adaptation Models

Altcoins in the gaming area could alter conventional adaptation models. Designers can involve these tokens for starting coin contributions (ICOs), empowering local area support and crowdfunding of gaming projects. Besides, players could procure tokens through ongoing interaction, contests, or adding to the game's turn of events, preparing for novel adaptation systems.

5. Challenges and Considerations

Be that as it may, this change isn't without its difficulties. Administrative worries, adaptability issues, and guaranteeing inescapable reception of blockchain innovation inside the gaming local area are huge obstacles. Finding some kind of harmony between the advantages of decentralization and the requirement for easy-to-use encounters will be basic in the far-reaching acknowledgement of gaming altcoins.

6. A Look into the Future

The eventual fate of gaming altcoins seems promising, imagining a scene where blockchain innovation consistently coordinates with the gaming experience. Gamers will have phenomenal command over their gaming resources and possibly partake in the creation and administration of the games they love. Cooperation between engineers, gamers, and blockchain devotees will be key in controlling this future, guaranteeing a harmonious relationship that expands the capability of gaming altcoins.

Gaming altcoins present an interesting possibility for the gaming business, promising a future where possession, decentralization, and creative adaptation models become the dominant focal point, reshaping how we see and cooperate with computer games. In any case, a wary and cooperative methodology is fundamental to exploring the difficulties and understanding the monstrous capability of this change in perspective.

Developments and forthcoming patterns forming the gaming altcoin scene. The gaming altcoin scene is quickly advancing, driven by different developments and arising patterns. Blockchain innovation, especially using non-fungible tokens (NFTs) and decentralized finance (DeFi), has essentially affected the gaming business.

1. NFT Joining in Gaming: Non-fungible tokens (NFTs) are exceptional computerized resources that can address in-game things, characters, or different components. NFT combination permits gamers to claim and exchange their in-game resources, cultivating another degree of proprietorship and worth inside the gaming biological system genuinely.

2. Play-to-Procure (P2E) Models: P2E models empower players to procure digital money by drawing in with and advancing inside a game. This could include finishing journeys, exchanging things, or partaking in competitions. It's a change in outlook from customary gaming where players went through hours with no monetary return.

3. Decentralized Gaming Platforms: Blockchain-based decentralized stages are arising, permitting engineers to make games with straightforward guidelines and mechanics. These stages influence savvy agreements to guarantee reasonableness and establish trustless gaming conditions.

4. Cross-Game Interoperability: A few undertakings are pursued permitting players to utilize resources across numerous games. This implies a thing procured in one game could be used in another, improving the general gaming experience and making a brought-together virtual economy.

5. Governance and Local area Involvement: Gaming altcoins progressively including the local area in dynamic cycles. Token holders can partake in administration recommendations, helping shape the eventual fate of the task and the games related to it.

6. Layer 2 Answers for Scalability: To address the adaptability challenges related to blockchain networks, Layer 2 arrangements like sidechains and rollups are being coordinated. These arrangements improve exchange speeds and lessen charges, critical for consistent gaming encounters.

7. Integration of computer-based intelligence and VR/AR: Man-made brainpower (simulated intelligence) is being utilized to upgrade game mechanics, adjust interactivity to individual players, and make more vivid encounters. Computer-generated Reality (VR) and Expanded Reality (AR) are likewise being incorporated to hoist gaming to another degree of submersion.

8. Carbon-Impartial Gaming Altcoins: With expanding natural worries, some gaming altcoins are zeroing in on eco-accommodating methodologies, going for the gold or counterbalancing their carbon impression through different drives.

These patterns altogether show the groundbreaking capability of blockchain and related advances in the gaming altcoin scene, offering new roads for the two engineers and gamers the same.

S. Hypotheses On How Gaming Altcoins Could Reclassify The Eventual Fate Of Gaming And Money.

Gaming altcoins, a type of digital money explicitly intended for the gaming business, can reform both gaming and money in more ways than one. First and foremost, they could present a decentralized economy inside games, permitting players to claim in-game resources and exchange them across various games and stages.

By using blockchain innovation, gaming altcoins could give straightforward and secure exchanges, decreasing misrepresentation and guaranteeing fair incentives for in-game things. Furthermore, players could acquire these altcoins through ongoing interaction accomplishments, competitions, or by adding to the gaming environment, accordingly making new roads for adaptation inside the gaming scene.

Moreover, gaming altcoins could empower cross-stage interoperability, allowing players to involve their procured resources in different games, improving the gaming experience and expanding player commitment. This could encourage the development of a virtual gaming economy where players can contribute, exchange, and make money inside the gaming biological system.

As far as money, gaming altcoins could obscure the lines between conventional money and gaming, making ready for inventive monetary items and administrations. Players could utilize these altcoins for credits, speculations, or even as security, making an extension between the gaming business and the more extensive monetary area.

Nonetheless, it's fundamental to think about the possible dangers, like market unpredictability, administrative difficulties, and the requirement for cautious incorporation to guarantee fair play and forestall abuse. The fruitful coordination of gaming altcoins will rely upon joint effort between game designers, blockchain specialists, and monetary organizations to make a maintainable and evenhanded gaming and monetary environment.

CONCLUSION

UNLOCKING THE VIRTUAL VAULT

Taking everything into account, unlocking the Virtual Vault holds colossal potential for changing how we oversee and get our computerized resources. By utilizing progressed encryption, multifaceted validation, and state-of-the-art network protection measures, we can guarantee the security and openness of delicate data put away inside the virtual domain. Embracing this innovation opens ways to improved information insurance, smoothed-out access, and eventually, a more productive and secure computerized scene. Nonetheless, it's essential to stay cautious and proactive in tending to arising difficulties and remaining refreshed with developing security guidelines to completely understand the advantages of opening the Virtual Vault.

SUMMING UP KEY FOCUS POINTS FROM THE BOOK

"Cryptogame Narratives: Divulging the Universe of Gaming Altcoins" digs into the convergence of digital money and gaming, investigating the arising domain of gaming altcoins. The book talks about the possible effect of these particular cryptographic forms of money on the gaming business, looking at their job in-game exchanges, resource proprietorship, and decentralized gaming biological systems. It reveals insight into how gaming altcoins could change player encounters, encouraging another time of financial open doors and cultivating a nearer joining of virtual and certifiable economies. The story underscores the significance of understanding this developing scene for both gaming fans and cryptographic money financial backers.

Empowering perusers to investigate the thrilling universe of gaming altcoins and imagine their prospects.

Absolutely! Gaming altcoins are an outright exhilarating wilderness in the consistently developing universe of cryptographic money. Envision is essential for a computerized transformation that combines the fervour of gaming with the potential for monetary development. These one-of-a-kind altcoins offer open doors to play your #1 games as well as be a partner in their turn of events. Dig into this invigorating domain, imagine the potential outcomes it holds, and consider the excursion of advancement and venture that looks for you. Embrace the eventual fate of gaming and crypto, where your enthusiasm for gaming can likewise fuel your monetary.

www.ingramcontent.com/pod-product-compliance
Lightning Source LLC
Chambersburg PA
CBHW071013260726
48661CB00007B/2932